Vol 1

THE PLEASANT ATHEIST
ADULT COLORING BOOK

A LOOK INSIDE NON-BELIEF IN 50 IMAGES

Judy Saint

THE PLEASANT ATHEIST ADULT COLORING BOOK A Look Inside Non-Belief in 50 Images

ABOUT THIS BOOK Graphics and imagery are gaining popularity as an effective learning medium, conveying information, emotions, and new experiences quickly in a fun way. Storytelling through pictures can often convey more than words filling a page. Combine that with the relaxing and often addictive coloring hobby which is also gaining popularity with adults, and you have the perfect tool to introduce a new and often counter-intuitive experience. Let Judy walk you through how she views life as an atheist, from the basics of daily living to feeling a transcendent awe and thankfulness so many of us share.

DISCLAIMER The author takes literary license at times to exaggerate or over-simplify to help communicate basic concepts, providing a starting point from which readers are invited to investigate further. Some views are United States-centric and Christian-centric because these are the experiences of the author but can be applied more broadly. The ideas presented, while generally typical, do not necessarily represent the views of all atheists, which is the beauty of non-belief. "Atheists are free to color their lives however they choose," as Dan Barker puts it, meaning not only this book, but our views on life as well.

BULK COPIES Bulk discounts are available as giveaways or for resale. Your organization's information labels can be adhered conveniently to the blank inside cover.

CONTACT
Email: Info@thepleasantatheist.com
Website with photo gallery: www.thepleasantatheist.com
YouTube: "The Pleasant Atheist Adult Coloring Book" features "Color with Judy" videos

Mint Tea Publishing, PO Box 2883, Rocklin, California 95677-8464
SAN 992-6429
ISBN 978-0-578-28627-3
First Edition

Image Concepts and Captions: Judy Saint
Illustrator: Evan Lilley

Copyright 2022 J Saint
All rights reserved. No part of this book may be used or reproduced in any manner whatsoever without written permission from the publisher and copyright holders. Requests should be mailed to the address above. PRINTED IN THE UNITED STATES OF AMERICA

A portion of all sales supports the Freedom From Religion Foundation.

Table of Contents
Section Themes

Question Everything	1
Things Change	3
Humans as an Adapting Animal	9
Morality in Other Adapting Animals	15
Morality and Doing Good	23
Trusting Atheists	37
Religious Understanding Among Atheists	39
Purpose, Meaning and Value of Life	41
It's OK to Not Know All the Answers	47
What's It Like to Be an Atheist?	49
How Atheists Celebrate Holidays and Traditions	57
Dealing with Difficulty	61
How Atheists Look at Prayer	63
Wishful Thinking for an Afterlife	67
Our Brains Are Obsessive Storytellers	69
Occam's Razor	75
Pascal's Wager	77
The Risk of Being Yourself	79
How Many Non-Religious People Are There?	81
Our Secular Governing	83
Our Place in the Universe	95
Imagine No Religion – It's Easy If You Try	99
My Journey to Non-Belief	101
Selected Resources and Links	102
About the Author, Links to Gallery and "Color With Judy"	103

Question Everything
"It's a healthy thing now and then to hang a question mark on things."
– Bertrand Russell

Traditions Change
It's OK to question traditions.

Religious Traditions Change
Can you believe Christmas was once outlawed in this country? It was. Today, of course, December 25th is a popular holiday. Long before Christmas, people called the middle of winter celebration by other names, such as Yule and Saturnalia.

Humans Change
Meet your new neighbors. Or they would be if all the dozens of other human species hadn't gone extinct. We are the one remaining human species.

Humans Are Not the Fastest Animal

Cheetahs go from 0 to 60 mph in 3 seconds. Humans can't run that fast. We are just another adapting animal, not "the best" at everything.

Humans Are Not the Strongest Animal
African elephants can carry the weight of a Tyrannosaurus Rex. Humans can't do that. We are just another adapting animal, not "the best" at everything.

Humans Do Not Have the Best Eyesight
Eagles see five times as far as humans, and that's without ever visiting an optometrist. Human animals can do some things best, but not everything. Humans are just another adapting animal.

Other Animals Show Fairness
Rats will rescue each other before eating the available chocolate.
(Not necessarily with ladders.)

Other Animals Also Show Empathy
Mice forgo treats if they know it hurts another mouse.

Other Animals Show Cooperation
Dolphins are known to distract hammerhead sharks to save human divers. Dolphins also guide lost whales back to open sea.

Other Animals Help the Needy
Younger chimps bring water to older arthritic chimps. (In their mouths, not pails.)
They also push them up trees to socialize and play cards. (OK, not to play cards.)
Other animals show morality without religion. Humans can, too.

Internal Morality Is Your Higher Power
How do you know which parts of biblical writings apply to us today and which parts don't? No one has to tell you we don't kill mouthy children anymore. You just know.
We all just know.

It Feels Good to Do Good
Knowing that people tend to do good gives us all real hope and optimism.
And sometimes new friends.

Helping Requires No Belief in Stories
People like to help when they can.

Some Help Is Organized
Many people organize to do good through their communities, societies, clubs, meetup groups, churches, youth sports leagues and other opportunities.

It's Up to Us
Atheists help others without a thought of anything supernatural.

"Do unto others as you would have them do unto you."
— The Golden Rule

FOUND EVERYWHERE

Egyptian Goddess Ma'at- 2000 BC

Code of Hammurabi- 1750 BC

Greece- 600 BC

Tamil Tradition- 500 BC

India Mahabharta- 400 BC

Persian Zoroastrianism- 300 BC

Many writings from long before the bible remind us to love one another, treat others fairly, use wisdom in judgment, and other reminders of our better natures.

You Can Trust Atheists the Same as Anyone
Integrity feels good, too, without rewards or threats. Integrity comes from who we are inside. Trust each person based on your experience with them, including atheists.

Atheists Know about Religions
Atheists tend to score higher than believers on tests of knowledge of religions.
That is why many say they are atheist – because they did study the books.

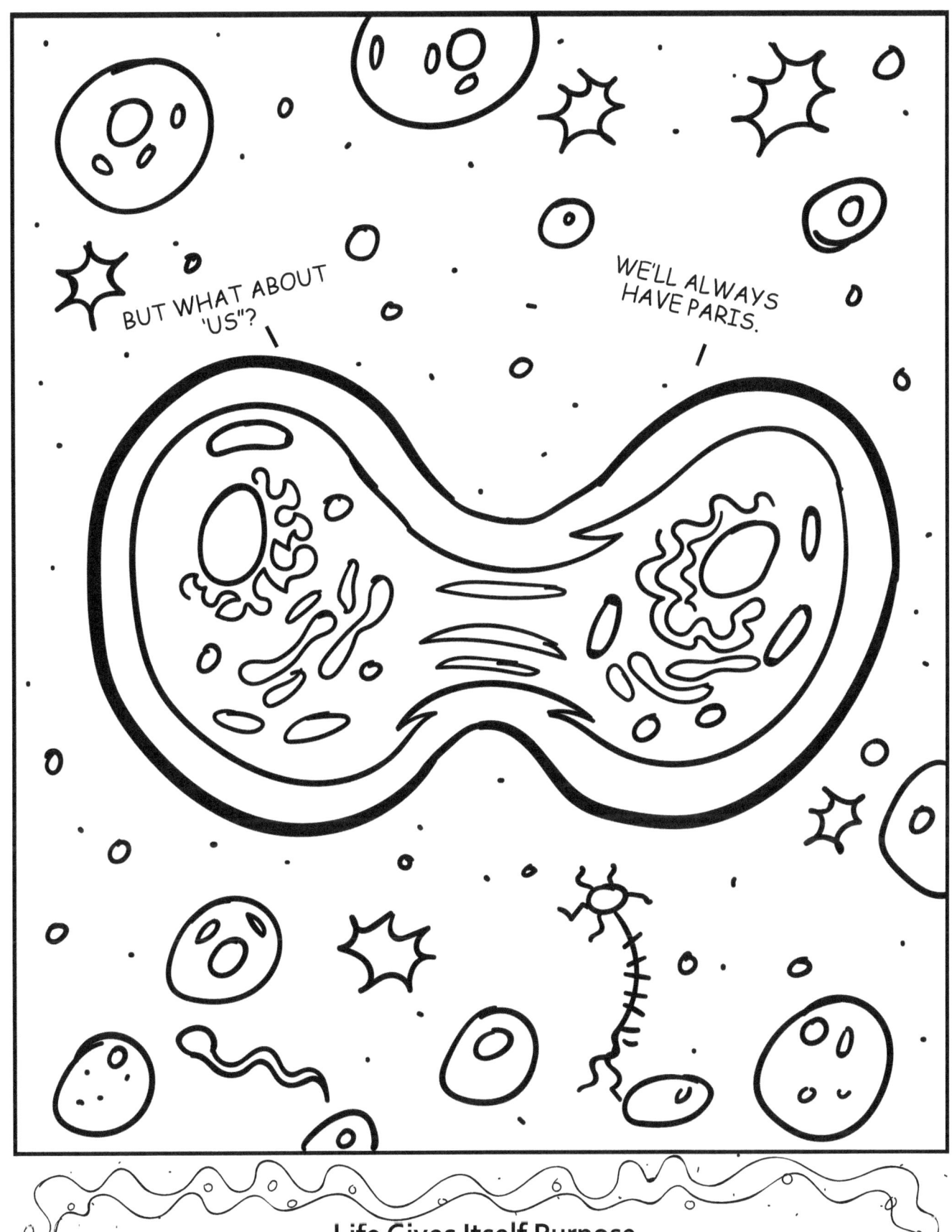

Life Gives Itself Purpose
Even if the inanimate universe exists with or without us, life forms do have a purpose: to survive, thrive and multiply. We would quickly go extinct without it. The purpose of life is more life.

"Life is a series of dogs" – George Carlin
The meaning of life is your choice. Hobbies, job, family, volunteering, love, learning, joy, leaving a legacy, or lots of pets. Finding your own meaning can fulfill you, even if it changes.

Life Is Precious to Atheists
If your beloved pet only had a few days left, you would treasure every minute.
That's how atheists view this life – as limited and precious.

It's OK to Not Know All the Answers
If atheists don't have the answer we can just say, "I don't know." And we're right.

Atheists Are Accepting
Atheists don't condemn anyone to hell because we don't believe in hell.
We have no ancient writings separating us from others.

Atheists Are Thankful
Atheists thank doctors, nurses, researchers, workers, farmers, parents, teachers, shopkeepers, brave leaders, friends and other real people.

Atheists Enjoy Good Stories
Atheists do not live their lives by ancient supernatural stories nor modern supernatural stories. Stories are just stories. Some are fun.

Atheists Are Practical
Want a bridge? Build one. Want to move a mountain? Find a shovel.
If you can't move a mountain by faith, maybe it's not your lack of faith.

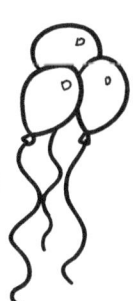

Atheists Celebrate Life Events

Weddings can have dancing, buffet, live music, wine bar, singing, fun videos, and signing a license – without any religious parts. The same is true for all life event gatherings. No religious parts are needed.

Atheists Celebrate Traditions
Many atheists celebrate traditional and religious holidays, usually out of nostalgia or to join the fun. Some don't, and that's OK too.

Trauma Is Real. Care Is Real.
Atheists might sit with you, listen, invite you to events, babysit, offer rides, pick up prescriptions, watch your pets, or any help that is real and appropriate.
It's OK to allow grief and healing to happen.

Beans Don't Hear Prayers
Beans just don't magically appear in starving childrens' hands.
Not even one bean.
If beans don't react to prayers, maybe nothing does.

Gravity Doesn't Hear Prayers
Falling planes and pianos just don't stop in mid-air.
If falling objects don't react to prayers, maybe nothing does.

Is There an Afterlife?
We all want to see our loved ones again. The wanting is real, but wanting does not make it true. Atheists appreciate passed loved ones in our hearts.

Our Brains Are Obsessive Storytellers
Our brains can turn any coincidence into a personal sign or comfort. It's easy to add meaning to anything. It can become an obsessive habit.

One-in-a-Million Coincidences
One-in-a-million coincidences happen around us all the time. What is unusual is when we notice one. What if a photo of a recently deceased loved one fell from a shelf? Our brains would want to make up stories immediately.

Supernatural Interpretations Add Nothing
If the situation would be the same with or without supernatural stories, why add the stories?

Occam's Razor
Why add extra supernatural layers to a situation when it does not change anything?
Shave off all unnecessary assumptions, said William of Occam.

Should We Believe "Just in Case"? (Pascal's Wager)
You would waste your life pretending to believe in all the gods just in case one is real. There have been thousands that people believed in, all with their own rules. You'd better get started. (But could you fool a god, anyway?)

The Risk of Being Yourself
It can be scary to not be what others want you to be. Many atheists lose relationships when they come out as atheist. However, according to studies, they're happier. Some experience unconditional acceptance for the first time.

There Are Many of Us
Atheists don't tend to speak up or organize, but we're here. Almost one-third of the people in the US are not affiliated with any religion.

Separation of Church and State
Our Constitution is a shield that protects your right to your belief,
but it is not a sword that can be used to force your belief on another.

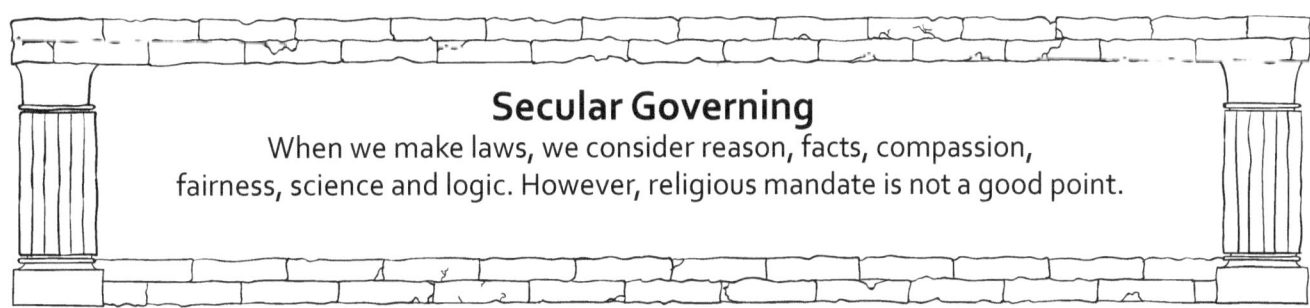

Secular Governing
When we make laws, we consider reason, facts, compassion,
fairness, science and logic. However, religious mandate is not a good point.

The Scientific Method Moves Us Forward
"Between science and religion, I choose the one that works."
– Stephen Hawking

Displays on Government Property

Religious displays on government property are OK if all religions are allowed equally, including atheist displays.

Prayers in Public Schools
Students can pray in public schools if no staff or public address systems are involved, and if it does not interfere with classes.

E Pluribus Unum
Our national motto was "E Pluribus Unum" (out of many, one) until 1956. Many want to change it back because it includes everyone and encourages unity.

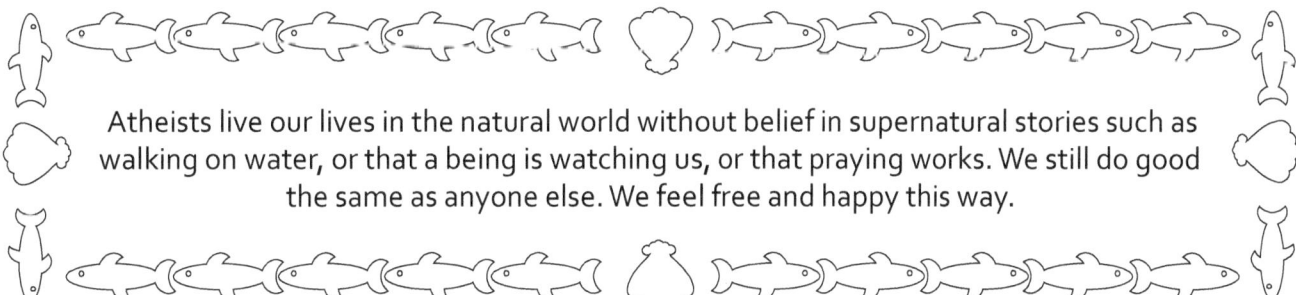

Atheists live our lives in the natural world without belief in supernatural stories such as walking on water, or that a being is watching us, or that praying works. We still do good the same as anyone else. We feel free and happy this way.

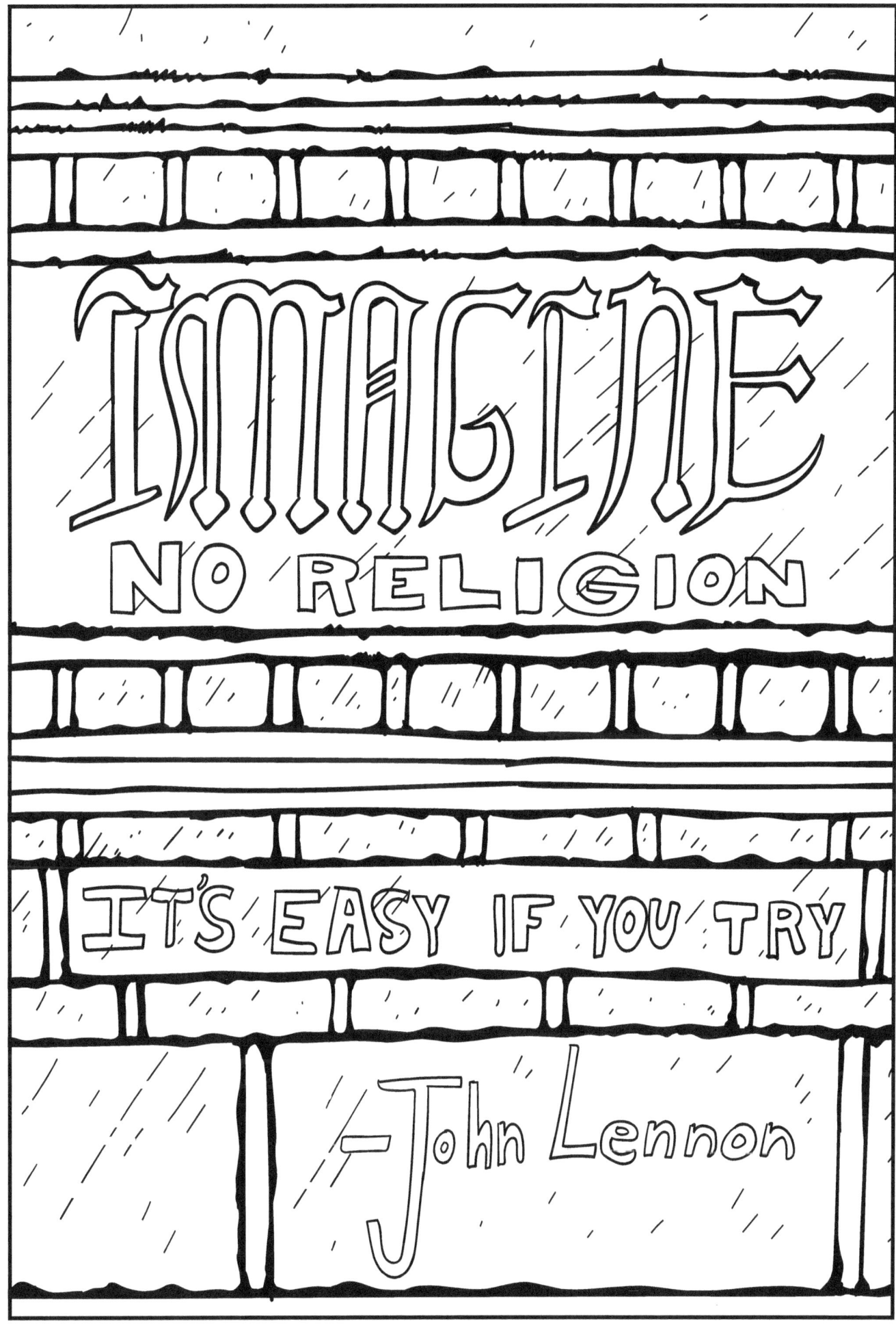

MY JOURNEY TO NON-BELIEF

Raised in a Protestant home, learning from my mother about faith and God's protection when things got tough, non-belief had never occurred to me. So, finding disturbing or even immoral passages as I read through my burgundy leather-covered bible over the years, I shrugged and accepted the idea of miracles and mysterious ways for five decades. In fact, just after I was baptized as an adult, I thumped my bible loud and clear, attending church every time the doors were open. This fervor faded over the next few decades, but not my faith that mountains really could be moved. I accepted the fact that I could not move any mountains myself, but maybe someday. It was just a matter of enough faith, I believed.

One day I had a question, "Who were the Pilgrims running away from?" I learned it was the opposite of what I had been taught in public school. The Pilgrims left England not because they had to hide in basements to pray, but because their local communities would not adopt their strict religious rules. The Pilgrims were not humble victims of an oppressive society; they were apparently the would-be oppressors. They came to the New World where they placed their strict religious rules into law, leading to imprisonment for disobedience and even shunning from the settlements, which at that time meant probable death. Interesting twist, I thought.

In reading about these events, something stunned me. Apparently, Christmas was outlawed in this country once. This seemed incredible. I learned Protestants hated Catholics, calling Christmas decorations "trappings of Popery." Well, it was not long before I found *Pagan Origins of the Christ Myth*, and off I went into serious fact-finding, after over 50 years of shrugging and accepting.

But, not so fast... We all still pray, don't we? I stopped right there, realizing I had never seen anything truly supernatural. I never heard of anything defying gravity or of a person's amputated limb growing back. I never heard of even one small bean appearing magically in a starving child's hand. Nothing supernatural. Just life, and good people doing good. But no magic. ... So, I had a new question: Does prayer even work?

Suddenly I thought not, which felt like a thud to the head. About a month later I had another thud-to-the-head realization that nothing would be any different if there were no god. "Is there even a god?" I asked myself. "Probably not," I thought. "There is no need to follow what has no effect," I concluded. I was done living according to theism. I felt freed from superstition and from religious judgment and guilt. The world seemed more colorful. My life was now my own.

I hope more people will see non-believers as we truly are – people who are basically the same as anyone else. "It's just the stories," I always say. "Atheists just don't believe the supernatural stories." Doing good, accepting others, and loving life are still my values, the same as before.

This book is a depiction of my personal experiences that brought me to non-belief. I hope you enjoy my journey in pictures that you can color for yourself. :-)

SELECTED RESOURCES

Organizations with More Resources For You

Freedom From Religion Foundation … https://www.ffrf.org

Greater Sacramento Chapter of FFRF … https://www.sac.ffrf.org

American Humanist Association … http://www.americanhumanist.org/

Recovering From Religion … https://www.recoveringfromreligion.org

The Clergy Project … https://www.clergyproject.org

Secular Coalition for America … https://www.secular.org (see *The Model Secular Policy Guide*)

Books

Coming Out Atheist by Greta Christina (numerous interviews of atheists who came out)

The Way of the Heathen: Practicing Atheism in Everyday Life by Greta Christina (gentle topics)

Pagan Origins of the Christ Myth by John G Jackson (fact-based history of similar christ stories)

Nailed by David Fitzgerald (well-researched evidence for and against a real Jesus Christ)

The God Delusion by Richard Dawkins (profound discussion of why so many believe)

Expose Yourself by Erin Louis (fun stories and inspiration to live life as yourself)

Any book or video by Frans de Waal

Podcasts, News and YouTube Channels

OnlySky … https://www.onlysky.media (news, entertainment, articles selected for atheists)

The Thinking Atheist … https://www.thethinkingatheist.com (engaging, polite discussions)

The Friendly Atheist … https://friendlyatheist.patheos.com (polite non-believer updates)

The Atheist Experience … https://www.axp.show (down-to-earth Q&A with believers)

DarkMatter2525 (YouTube Channel that educates with humor and animated cartoons)

NonStampCollector (YouTube channel that makes its points simply)

Underlings (YouTube channel with serious analysis from a pleasant, knowledgeable guy)

How to Find Local Freethinking Groups

Meetup.com (search for freethought, non-belief, or atheist groups near you)

Google.com (search for freethought or "atheist groups near me")

Look for local chapters of national freethought and human rights organizations

The Best Resource of All

Letting yourself ask questions

View Gallery

Color with Judy

ABOUT THE AUTHOR

Judy Saint is a public school educator, textbook author, bass player, computer programmer, black belt, business owner, photographer, National Merit Scholar, flew her own plane across the country, rides a Harley with a sidecar for her German Shepherd, has several college degrees (Mathematics, Psychology, Curriculum Development and Educational Leadership), and is mother of two accomplished grown children.

Following instructions to "Stay as sweet as you are" by everyone, she says, who signed her high school yearbook, she accepts that as validation that she is indeed a pleasant atheist.

Ms. Saint lives in California.

www.ingramcontent.com/pod-product-compliance
Lightning Source LLC
Chambersburg PA
CBHW051213290426
44109CB00021B/2443